25 WAYS TO CONTROL YOUR STAGE FRIGHT—
AND BECOME A HIGHLY CONFIDENT SPEAKER

INTRODUCTION:

At the outset, note that the title said *control* your stage fright, not *eliminate* that fear, which many people would love to do. Why do I take this approach? Because having a moderate amount of stage fright is beneficial, reflecting that you are "up for the occasion," charged, energetic, concerned. Often I tell my coaching clients they wouldn't want to go to an athletic event, such as a football game, and see the players yawning before the game starts.

While noting the advantages that a moderate level of stage fright brings, I am writing this e-book to help those among us—of any age or profession—who become terrified at the thought of facing an audience. In extreme cases, these individuals:

--refuse opportunities for civic leadership
--accept where they are professionally instead of seeking advancement
--remain silent on issues where they have strong convictions

You might wonder whether I have ever felt extreme stage fright. Answer: many times. Examples:

--My first meeting with the class I taught in the Atlanta Federal Penitentiary
--My first keynote address at a convention
--Telling a selection committee why I was the ideal candidate for the job
--The first hour with a new group of university students during my faculty days

Fortunately, during my faculty, then management, and then consulting careers, I developed *a stage fright control system that works well* for me. Not only that, my approach has helped hundreds of clients at all levels. So I know that when you follow my guidelines, you too will greatly increase the odds of becoming a poised, confident speaker.

Amazingly, you—like many of my clients—may very well not only start enjoying speaking engagements that come your way. . .you'll even seek them yourself!

Now for the *25 ways to control your stage fright*, and become the presenter you have dreamed about becoming.

ONE: ALLOW AMPLE TRAVEL TIME TO THE EVENT
I offer this tip at the outset because you might not have realized how upset you will become if you are fighting the clock on the way to the event. Also, you never know what surprises you might have along the way: car trouble, road construction delays, rush hour traffic jams, a flat tire, or even getting lost despite the electronic devices you rely on.

Allow for all these contingencies by padding your schedule with far more travel time than you would allow if you were a participant instead of the speaker.

Stated more positively, arriving well ahead of your speech reduces your anxiety because you greet the meeting planners and audience members who start drifting in. Further, you become familiar with the meeting room. Equally important, you can casually check the microphones, PowerPoint, and other support items.

One more consideration: after checking the speech setting and meeting some attendees, you will relax more when you have an opportunity to leave the building, if the weather allows, and stroll around casually for a few minutes. Light exercise and fresh air foster the serenity you need.

TWO: START YOUR SPEECH WITH SOMETHING EASY
To control the situation right away, don't begin with something complicated. Neither you nor the audience is ready for an intricate discussion about complex issues.

Rather, begin with a relevant-to-the-topic two or three minutes of content you can deliver with the ease you'd have talking with a friend you take a coffee break with. For instance: An interesting experience that happened to you or somebody else catches attention, and demands very little memorizing or visual aids.

THREE: DON'T START BY TELLING A JOKE
There are several good reasons for avoiding jokes, even though common practice

suggests that most speakers think jokes will automatically establish rapport with the audience. Consider these problems with telling jokes:

--In the age of the Internet, you might have trouble telling a joke your listeners have not heard or read already.
--Most jokes have a "fall" guy, and you could offend someone who fits that category, or even someone sympathetic to the group you are jesting about.
--Successful joke telling requires perfect timing, supporting facial expressions, and emphasis on the right words.

Most importantly, jokes are risky because if the speaker fails to deliver the joke convincingly, both the speaker and the audience will become very uncomfortable. Regaining your composure and the audience's attention (and respect in some cases) is difficult.

Now please understand that I am not against humor in your opening remarks. Instead of trying to make a punch line work, take an option that works more effectively. Use self-deprecating humor, poking fun at yourself good naturedly. Or even use a spontaneous quip that comes to mind.

For safety's sake, leave the jokes to the late night comedians. They appear on TV because they have mastered the art.

Here again, by following this tip you will reduce your tension, since you don't have to silently wonder, "What if they don't get the joke?"

FOUR: USE GOOD SPEAKING HABITS DAILY
By using good speaking habits in everyday conversation, you won't have to make radical changes when you share ideas with your audience.

This point reminds me of Ed McMahon, the longtime partner of Johnny Carson, host of The Tonight Show, which was immensely popular on late night TV for decades. McMahon told a reporter, "I never use foul language off camera, because I want to stay completely away from language that would offend my television audience."

Beyond using clean language in your business and social interactions, form the habit of enunciating clearly. Become a keen listener, for that skill will help you in the question and answer session following your speech. Sense how people are responding to you in casual situations, training you to read the reactions of your audience.

FIVE: AVOID TAKING UPPERS AND DOWNERS
"I need to get revved up, so I'll gulp down three or four cups of coffee before the event starts." Wrong! Why? Because we are stimulated enough already. Caffeine will magnify our heightened state, possibly leading to nervous jitters.

I have had novice speakers tell me, "A little whiskey will calm my nerves." That's another mistake! Stay away from beverages or pills you believe would relax you. Example: Many of my convention meeting planners host cocktail receptions an hour or so before convening the group for my keynote speech. I assure you, though the alcoholic beverages are free and usually give me choices of premium brands, I stick with a glass of water or a soft drink. Even "one drink just to be social" might weaken your memory and cause you to slur words. Far better to have a celebration drink afterward, maybe in the privacy of your hotel room.

SIX: DON'T TRY TO BE PURRRFFFFICT
Yes, I misspelled *perfect* intentionally because I wanted you to see that it's OK to make a mistake. You still knew what I meant, didn't you? Now the good news is that audiences will get what you mean and understand you clearly even though you make a bobble or two here and there. For instance, occasionally you will:

--mispronounce some words
--stammer or stutter, even though that's not your habit
--skip a slide in your PowerPoint
--drop a book you were holding up to recommend
--lose your place temporarily

Well so what? In every instance, these few seconds are only a fraction of the time you are speaking.

Even more significantly, realize that audiences don't expect—and certainly don't want—a flawless speaker. Haven't you heard this description of a speaker after the event?

"She just phoned it in."

Interpret that to mean she was robotic, mechanical, devoid of the blunders and bloopers listeners expect you to make. Oh yes, she was flawless. Give her Grade A for that. Yet that's not entirely commendable, because that's not the way we communicate winsomely.

Here's a suggestion: Go to You Tube and type in "broadcast bloopers." You'll see many dozens of clips that show top professional newscasters pronouncing words wrong, inverting words, and even slipping into accidental profanity. You see, if even the highest paid and best trained reporters can't speak perfectly, then why should you put pressure on yourself to deliver an error-free speech?

This may prompt you to wonder, "If I am destined to speak imperfectly, what should I do when I falter?" Simple answer: nothing. Don't give it any attention, either internally or vocally. Realize you have just proved your humanity, which audiences respond to very positively.

Sure, this thought takes getting used to. From childhood, adults, teachers, mentors, and bosses encourage us to be our best, even our "personal best" as we started hearing a couple of years ago. Yet *best* does not imply *perfect*.

Why did golf fans flock to professional Arnold Palmer starting in the 1950s and then remain rabid fans long after he won his last PGA Tour tournament in 1973? As you know, his massive gallery earned the designation "Arnie's Army." They stayed because they could identify with an immensely talented player who missed shots just like they did. Many times Palmer took chances that didn't work, meaning he had to hit his next shot from deep grass, behind tall trees, and in cavernous bunkers.

Go ahead, then, miss some shots when you speak. Strive to share your ideas with your audience energetically, entertainingly, emotionally, and authoritatively of course.

But forget being perfect.

Are we connected on LinkedIn? If not, please send me an invitation:
https://www.linkedin.com/in/billlampton

SEVEN: CHANGE YOUR OPINION ABOUT AUDIENCES
We have just noted that audiences will tolerate—and surprisingly even welcome—your flaws and foibles. This observation leads me to recommend that you not accept the traditional opinion most speakers have about audiences. You might hear some of these comments:

"They are so critical."

"They will judge me harshly."

"Hard to hold their attention, they will start texting soon."

"When I ask them to interact, they'll probably sit there stone-faced."

Popular as these sentiments are, take heart in knowing they are inaccurate. Really, *audiences want you to succeed.* After all, when a speaker fails the audience becomes just as uncomfortable and embarrassed as the presenter.

I like to tell my coaching clients and my seminar audiences that there's one main thought going through the minds of the people I speak to: "Gosh, I am glad Bill is the one up there speaking, and not me!"

Therefore, shift your mental image of the audiences you are going to face. They are not your *critics*. They are your *cheerleaders*.

Not only do they accept your imperfections, they will endure instances when your train of thought appears to have left the track. They will allow you a misstated fact or quotation, as long as they know you weren't generally careless in your research.

Here's where I get a bit perturbed at egotistical speakers who brag, "Man, I scored big with that audience." These self-appointed superstars assume the speech was a hit solely because of the speaker's wit, expertise, and charisma. A more accurate reflection would be to give plenty of credit to the audience for making the speaker feel accepted.

Next time you speak, say a silent "thank you" for those *cheerleaders* who want you to succeed from every standpoint. This will reduce your stage fright immeasurably.

EIGHT: YOU'VE GOT THE TRUMP CARD
Except for a few times I played card games in my fraternity house just to be social, I've never been one to play bridge, poker, canasta, and other table games very often. But even though I am not an expert at cards, I do know that in some games having the "trump card" is a big advantage, greatly increasing your likelihood of winning.

This is why I tell speakers, "Remember, you have the trump card." *What is that trump card?* This: Prior to your speech, you and you alone know what you intend to say. After your speech, you and you alone know what you meant to say.

Recall how many times you have given a speech, and then spent the hour during your drive home agonizing over some fact or story you failed to include, or a wrong date you gave about an event. No need for that—only you are aware of the omission or misstatement.

Another comforting thought: During your speech you don't need to get upset if you realize you skipped a story or statistic you wanted to use. Nobody knows but you!

This line of thought reminds me of a TV program named "I've Got a Secret." And you do. The secret is your content outline, whether the outline appears on paper or just resides in your mind. Since no one has access to your outline, you are free to depart from it radically, as long as you appear organized, logical, and in control.

Only actors must follow a script word-for-word. Speakers have the opportunity to omit, improvise, alter, and create as they feel the need.

Isn't it nice to know you are not being evaluated on what you had planned to say?

NINE: STAGE FRIGHT SYMPTOMS ARE PERSONAL, NOT PUBLIC
Jot down the symptoms of stage fright you experience before you speak—or even when you picture yourself giving a speech.

Your list could very well include:

--butterflies in the stomach
 --sweaty palms
--shaking knees
--quivering voice
--temporary memory lapse
 --dry mouth
 --extreme self-consciousness.

Consider: These symptoms are quite annoying to you, even alarming. You're afraid that everyone who is watching you knows what is happening with you physically. That fear compounds your anxiety.

Consider also: *Your tremors and trepidation are not visible to others*, unless you faint and have to be carried out of the room. . .which I have never seen happen.

Want proof that your symptoms remain invisible to others? Then arrange to give a 3-5 minute speech on any topic that a colleague, family member, or Speech Coach video records for you. Watch the replay. What a relief you will feel when you get confirmation that the jitters that made you so uncomfortable were not detectable, even though you were looking for them. Far more than you predicted, you appeared in control.

TEN: PREPARATION REDUCES PERSPIRATION
One of my vastly talented high school classmates with the colorful name Eagle Day played college football at the University of Mississippi, more widely known as Ole Miss. During his years as quarterback the Rebels compiled an outstanding

record: twenty-six wins, five losses, and one tie. In an era when only four bowl games existed, Eagle's team played in the Sugar Bowl and the Cotton Bowl.

Throughout his lifetime we remained close friends. Once I asked him: "Eagle, I often help clients confront their stage fright, so it will be helpful for me to know how you kept your composure before such huge crowds—75,000 in the Cotton Bowl and 83,000 in the Sugar Bowl. What formula did you have for staying calm?"

Without hesitation he answered: "Bill, every day at practice I was the first player to arrive and the last one to leave. The night before every big game I stayed up late making sure that I knew our 150 offensive plays thoroughly. And I had to know how to adjust each of those plays when the defense moved into an unexpected formation."

His next sentence summed up how he directed his team confidently before massive crowds, including a vast TV audience:

"We won the game before we ever got to the stadium."

His explanation prompts me to observe, "The greater our *preparation*, the less *perspiration* we'll have."

Preparation might involve:

  --interviewing experts on your topic
  --reading articles and books by recognized authorities
  --watching educational videos
  --enlisting the services of a Speech Coach
--sharing your outline with a valued adviser
--adding photos and clip art to your *PowerPoint*
--practicing aloud once or twice on video

I chuckle when I remember the freshmen I taught in the basic speech course at the University of Georgia. Now and then, a few of them *deserved their fear*. Instead of preparing, they had enjoyed the collegiate social scene a bit too much the previous night or two. Meanwhile, their fellow students who prepared diligently demonstrated poise and confidence as a result of their research and planning.

ELEVEN: NEVER TALK TO STRANGERS
Our parents had our safety in mind when they told us, "Never talk to strangers."

For a different twist on those words of caution, I recommend that you never talk to strangers when you are giving a speech. Make sure you arrive early enough to get well acquainted with your host. Without abbreviating the getting acquainted time with the host, move tactfully to the point where you ask him or her to introduce you to some of the attendees as they drift into the room. Usually the corporate officers, meeting planners, and other leaders will arrive first. These are key people to connect with.

Initiate conversations with your new acquaintances. You can ask them about their responsibilities with the company. Or you can discuss upcoming or previous major events in the area, such as an athletic event or concert.

The happy result: After your host introduces you, you are not talking to strangers. In the audience you see a half dozen or more people who are now likely to support you visually. Additionally, when you ask for questions or discussion these are the ones who will support you verbally by responding.

TWELVE: PREPARE A CHECKLIST AND FOLLOW IT CLOSELY
Have you ever gone to a speaking engagement and realized, "I forgot to bring my bio sketch for the host to read while introducing me?" Understandably, your tension escalates.

To avoid that problem, think of what pilots do before every flight. They go over a checklist of each step involved in assuring a safe takeoff and flight. Although they might have looked at this list hundreds of times, they don't risk heading down the runway until they have put a checkmark by every procedural item.

Your speaking checklist could read like this, in part:
--3 thumb drives with PowerPoint presentation

--extra copy of introduction (the host might have forgotten what you sent)

--enough handouts

--business cards

--extra batteries for technical equipment

--copies of your speech outline

--pocket comb or brush

So you won't have to re-write the list every time, file a copy on your computer and print it as you start packing.

When you know you have brought every essential item with you, you will have much less to worry about.

Let's become Facebook friends:

https://www.facebook.com/doclampton

THIRTEEN: CHANGE YOUR SELF TALK

I advise clients, "Before you talk with your audience, first have a good pep talk with yourself."

Do these examples of self talk mirror what you habitually say to yourself just before you stand to speak?

"Last time I spoke to an audience I failed miserably."

"This group has so many good presenters in it, bet they will consider me a rank amateur."

"Too bad I didn't work on this speech enough. I'm practically winging it."

"Wish somebody else was doing this. I'm not right for this audience."

If those self-talk examples remind you of your silent internal musings on the day of your speech—then you have set yourself up for failure or at best mediocrity. Self-incriminating thoughts generate a defeatist attitude, leading to a subpar presentation.

Here's what to say inwardly, *and really mean it:*

"Sharing my ideas with this group is a great opportunity. I can hardly wait for the preliminaries to end, so the host will introduce me."

"Wow, I've made so much progress in my speaking skills in the last couple of years. I used to lose sleep the night before the event, but now I rest well because I know I can handle the challenge very capably."

"These people need my message. They will benefit tremendously. I am thrilled about serving them this way."

FOURTEEN: LEAVE "DELIVERY" TO FEDEX AND UPS

Although the term "speech delivery" remains widespread, I recommend that we ditch that description of speechmaking. Leave delivery to FedEx, UPS, and others who specialize in getting packages from one locale to another.

My thinking here: those jobs are quite methodical. Delivery personnel can take packages to homes or businesses without knowing or even seeing the recipients, and of course they did not furnish the content. Leaving the packages on porches and doorsteps completes the transaction.

Instead of "speech preparation and delivery," I encourage you to envision "speech preparation and conversation." Yes, that's right: *conversation.*

Your speaking—when you are at your best—strongly resembles a conversation with your audience. You say something, and you see them react to your words. In many cases, you will invite feedback, either during a ten minute question/answer session at the end, or anytime somebody wants to ask a question or offer an opinion.

The closer you move toward thinking of speaking as conversation, the calmer you will become. You are not the whole show. You have a sizable supporting cast.

Approach the speaking situation with the same comfort you feel when you chat with a friend you happen to see in the grocery store. The major difference, naturally, is that your speech requires extensive preparation, while the grocery store remarks will be impromptu. Even so, this is a helpful analogy to keep in mind.

Main point: Dynamic speeches progress well beyond monologue and feature considerable dialogue.

FIFTEEN: PUT YOUR SPEECH IN PROPER PERSPECTIVE

To begin with, if you heard a speech three weeks ago, do you remember the name of the speaker? What was her topic? What were two or three of her main points? What did she try to achieve?

Chances are good that those details have slipped out of your memory. Now suppose the speaker had thought, "This speech could make or break my reputation, even my career." Obviously, she exaggerated the consequences or benefits of her thirty minutes with your group.

A related question: How many speeches are you aware of in your lifetime that have truly changed history, or at least started those changes? John F. Kennedy's inaugural address? Martin Luther King's "I Have a Dream" speech?

Can you think of others to add to the list? If so, I wouldn't expect more than one or two.

This observation tells us that putting our speech in proper perspective will reduce our stress. Lincoln erred in saying the world would "little note nor long remember" his Gettysburg address. However, that phrase could well describe the overwhelming majority of our speeches.

No, I am not downplaying the significance of what you say to audiences. I am merely suggesting that you not consider the occasion a do-or-die hour.

SIXTEEN: SMILE—GENUINELY

Traditionally, we have assumed that we smile as a *result* of a feeling. Something has made us happy—compliment from our boss, good golf score, birthday wishes from friends, or our dream vacation. That traditional approach has held sway for centuries.

Recent research, though, indicates that the reverse happens, too. *The facial expression can cause the feeling.* Turn your lips down long enough, and sadness follows. Grit your teeth firmly, and you will sense hostility. Frown, and you will experience confusion.

Knowing this, you will enrich your mood by smiling throughout most of your speech—not as an actor, but *smiling genuinely*. You'd depart from that, of course, if you start talking about a somber matter, such as the severe illness of a friend.

One more benefit beyond minimizing your apprehension: When you smile constantly, your audience will feel more serenity, too. The smiling speaker appears authoritative and confident.

SEVENTEEN: PROMOTE AUDIENCE INTERACTION

The era of passive audiences expired. Your audience members are not content with merely listening, they want to become active participants.

Please note that this does not call for using trite, overworked instructions such as, "Oh come on now, you can say 'Good Morning' louder than that!" Avoid the all-too-common (and boring) calls to action you have heard before.

Be creative. Stimulate imaginations. Invite your audience to participate in relevant, productive interaction. Example "Working with the group at your table, take five minutes to list the top five providers of customer service you have dealt with. After you have done that, each table will appoint a leader who identifies the companies you selected."

What does this technique have to do with stage fright? Well, you get a breather. While the groups are at work, you can walk around or even leave the room for a couple of minutes. Take a sip of water. Stretch your arms. Yawn—which you would not want to do while speaking!

Definitely, the interaction helps the audience, too. As long-ago comedian Jimmy Durante said, "Everybody wants to get into the act." Also, the discussion will generate some ideas that become "keepers" for the participants.

So the double advantage is that when you resume talking, you feel refreshed and your audience feels recharged.

Visit my Speech Coaching Web site:
http://www.championshipcommunication.com

EIGHTEEN: BE AUTHENTIC

Jan Fox—an award winning television anchor, now a widely respected speech coach—talked about chatting with a group of professional speakers informally at a table near the stage where they would soon speak. To her disappointment, when one speaker moved from the group to the podium, he abandoned the conversational tone he had used naturally at the table. Suddenly, he used a "broadcast voice," possibly imitating one of his favorite on air personalities.

In her coaching, Jan prompts her clients to "be authentic." Your voice, she underscores, does not need embellishment.

Another renowned speech coach, who worked with nationally known speakers, said that his most effective clients sounded exactly the same regardless of the setting or size of the audience.

Generations ago, Ralph Waldo Emerson cautioned, "Imitation is suicide." Just be yourself at your best. With a large audience you might increase your volume to make sure you're heard, yet that doesn't call for changing your vocal style.

NINETEEN: MOVE AROUND

We have seen speakers who clung to the lectern as tightly as they would have held a life preserver if they had been passengers on the doomed Titanic. Not surprisingly, their fixed (or maybe I should say frozen) position did nothing to calm their nerves.

Yes, becoming freed from a lectern or a table where you have spread your notes and visual aids doesn't happen easily. By nature, most of us like that comfort zone. So you might not become highly mobile instantly. Even so, start somewhere. Next time you speak, take several steps away from your base. Eventually, you will enjoy the freedom of walking to the back row and saying to those seated there, "Bet you didn't expect to see me this close up!"

As you become more mobile with your feet, in all likelihood your gestures will become less rigid and confined.

TWENTY: DON'T FRET ABOUT GESTURES

"What should I do with my hands?" Coaching clients ask me that frequently. Usually I answer by reminding them of what I said earlier: speaking at its best bears a striking resemblance to conversation.

With that in mind, picture a conversation you had with a friend recently, possibly while you shared coffee or a meal. How much planning did you give to the gestures you were going to make? None, I'm sure. You gestured naturally and freely, your motions flowing spontaneously from what you were feeling when you spoke.

Let's say you were telling your friend about a sad event in your family. Probably you were quiet and rather still. At the opposite end, if you talked about a new child born into your family, my guess is you were highly animated as you showed photos and talked about the joy your family was having.

In other words, never plan or can gestures. Just let them happen.

The only other guideline I will offer about gestures is that you will want to become aware of gestures that might be awkward, or that are so repetitive they distract listeners. How do you identify gestures you can improve or eliminate? Give a ten minute speech that a colleague or coach records on video. Watch the playback carefully, at least twice. You might be pleasantly surprised that no gesture problems appear. If you see some, though, you can make a note to break those habits, so audiences will concentrate totally on your message.

TWENTY-ONE: CHOOSE THE BEST PREPARATION METHOD

The *Impromptu Method* allows for no preparation. Obviously, you will not choose to merely "wing it" when you have time to prepare. Occasionally you will speak spontaneously. Example: In a staff meeting, your CEO says, "You attended that conference last week. Tell us two or three helpful things you learned." To do that, you gather your thoughts quickly, and realize that no one expects eloquence, just accuracy.

The *Manuscript Method* represents an outdated way of preparing presentations—writing the speech out in full, with the intent of giving those words verbatim to the audience. As you can guess, the speaker in most cases seemed robotic, distant, and inflexible. Fortunately, the vast majority of presenters know that speaking from a manuscript is obsolete—and obnoxious.

The *Memorization Method* has the speaker memorizing the manuscript, and slavishly sticking to the text without notes while speaking. Put simply, memorizing belongs to actors, and no one else. Depending on flawless memory and recitation adds immensely to your already ample state of uneasiness.

The *Key Ideas and Key Words* method works far better than the other three. After you engage in extensive research—which can include interviews with experts—you start outlining your address by jotting down key ideas and words. Illustration:

"story about my weight loss"
"sensible nutrition changes"
"help from physical trainer"
"no overnight miracles"
"joy of fitting new wardrobe"

With this method, you are not bound to exact wording, and you are free to improvise during your speech when something relevant comes to mind.

As is the case with most habit changes, this switch could seem awkward at first. Stick with it, though, and you will step to the lectern with a spring in your step and abundant energy, since you have not spent hours in scriptwriting and oral rehearsals.

TWENTY-TWO: SELECT THE PROPER FOCUS

You have three choices about where you should focus your attention while speaking.

One focus choice is the audience. You aim to catch their attention and hold it. You want to inform, educate, and even entertain them. You make every effort to involve listeners actively.

Another focus choice is the topic. You believe ardently in the value of your message, and you want others to share your enthusiasm. Throughout your speech, nothing sways you from this dominant purpose.

A third focus choice is yourself. In this case, you have become absorbed with the impression you are making. Every minute, thoughts like these run through your mind:

"Are they liking me?"

"Why does that lady in the second row look bored?"

"One person left the room. Did he just need a break, or did I offend him?"

"Gosh, I just said 'uh' again. Talking like a real beginner!"

By now you know my strong recommendation. *Focus entirely on your topic and your audience.* Forget about the impression you are making. As you become one hundred per cent involved in helping audiences by giving them vital tips and strategies—and as you remove your ego from the scene—an unprecedented calm will embrace you.

Visit my "Biz Communication" Web site:
http://www.bizcommunicationguy.com

TWENTY-THREE: RUN TOWARD SPEAKING OPPORTUNITIES

Our natural—and understandable—tendency is to avoid stressful situations, especially those we fear the most. Consequently, in regard to speaking we might turn down invitations to make presentations. Yes, that protects us from upsetting challenges—but avoidance takes away chances to become more acclimated and more comfortable standing before audiences.

Instead of running away from speaking engagements, *run toward them*. Take initiative. Examples:

--Volunteer for a leadership role in a community organization

--Accept the chairmanship of a committee at work

--Make the rounds of civic clubs as a guest speaker

--Lead a fundraising drive for a charitable cause

Even professional speakers benefit from frequent speaking. Every time I speak, I gain more of an "I belong here" feeling.

TWENTY-FOUR: REMEMBER WHY YOU WERE INVITED TO SPEAK
Once in awhile someone invites a friend to speak, just because of the friendship. That's quite rare, though. Most of the time a group invites you to speak because they consider you highly qualified to handle the subject.

Think about that as you are making your way to the podium. A program chairman, selection committee, or a meeting planner believes that you are well-informed, maybe even what we call a "thought leader" in your arena. Well, if that's their opinion, why would you want to think less of your ability?

TWENTY-FIVE: SPEAK FROM THE PASSION IN YOUR HEART
One CNN staffer, anchor Brooke Baldwin, recalled her biggest TV blooper and then drew from her calamity a lesson about how to speak.

Before she came to CNN in 2008, she served an apprenticeship in smaller markets, including Charlottesville, Virginia. As Baldwin remembered, once in Charlottesville she experienced a "deer in the headlights" moment on camera. She was standing outside a jail, dozens of people were shouting at her, and she was going through the final steps of memorizing what she was going to report. Then when the camera started to roll, her mind went blank. In all the commotion, she forgot everything she had meticulously scripted. Red-faced, she stared silently into the camera. She assumed that she earned a few seconds on a highlight edition of worst bloopers of the year.

Yet she used what she had learned from that scary incident to advise iReporters-- ordinary citizens who submit brief reports for CNN's consideration. Brooke advised them to refrain from "spitting out everything you have memorized when you describe the scene or the pictures you are submitting." Exact wording and perfect diction are far are less important than *the passion we will hear in your voice.*"

In other words, the more deeply committed you are to your topic, the less attention you will give to your nervousness.

I purposely chose this as the twenty-fifth tip, because I value this approach greatly.

CONCLUSION:

Now that you have read my 25 favorite tips and strategies for controlling your stage fright, my prediction is that you will bolster your poise and confidence tremendously by applying these recommendations. As you have noticed, none of them are complicated nor do they involve a price tag, other than the investment of your time and thought.

To learn more about my Speech Coaching, I invite you to visit my Web site:

http://www.championshipcommunication.com

Note that you will be able to subscribe to my online newsletter, "Winning Words and Ways," by entering your name and address in the designated slots.

Additionally, this next Web site says more about my consulting with corporations:

http://www.bizcommunicationguy.com

Also, my LinkedIn profile reflects my broader range of services:

http://www.linkedin.com/in/billlampton

If we aren't connected there already, please send me an invitation.

Let's become Facebook friends: https://www.facebook.com/doclampton

And be sure to "Like" my Facebook business page!

https://www.facebook.com/Dr.BillLamptonCommunicationConsultant/

CONTACT ME!

To discuss your communication problems, and how I will help you overcome them, please call me—today:

678-316-4300

Keep in mind that I help you use. . .

the right words

the right way

to get

the right results!

Bill Lampton, Ph.D.

"Biz Communication Guy"

ABOUT THE AUTHOR

Bill Lampton earned his Ph.D. at Ohio University, and then taught Speech Communication at the University of Georgia—where he started helping speakers take control of their stage fright and speak with newfound confidence.

Dr. Lampton spent twenty-two years in management at the vice presidential level. Often he watched supervisors perform far short of their potential because they were fearful when they directed departmental meetings.

In 1997, he launched his company, Championship Communication. He has served as the keynote speaker for numerous conventions, directed seminars, and provided individual coaching to help leaders learn to speak confidently, clearly, and convincingly.

His top-tier client list includes:
Gillette
Procter and Gamble
Duracell
Missouri Bar
University of Georgia Athletic Association
British Columbia Legal Management System
Celebrity Cruises
Ritz-Carlton Cancun
Mississippi Division of Tourism
Krystal Company
Sage
National Parks Association
Environmental Protection Agency

A widely published author of communication articles, he wrote a popular book:
The Complete Communicator: Change Your Communication, Change Your Life!

The Gwinnett Chamber of Commerce in suburban Atlanta, Georgia named Championship Communication "Business of the Month" for July 2016.

Not surprisingly, Bill has earned this description: "Biz Communication Guy"

In addition to his communication coaching for corporations and individuals, he is available for voice over opportunities, a natural follow up to his decades as a freelance radio host.